114   636.1

A PONY CLUB PUBLICATION

The Foot and Shoeing

THE BRITISH HORSE SOCIETY
and THE PONY CLUB

© 1989 The British Horse Society

All rights reserved.
No part of this publication may be
reproduced, stored in a retrieval
system, or transmitted in any form or
by any means, electronic, mechanical,
photocopying, recording or otherwise
without the prior permission of The
British Horse Society.

British Library Cataloguing in Publication Data
The Foot and shoeing.—2nd ed.
    1. Farriery
    I. Pony Club Advisory Panel
    682'.1

    ISBN 0-900226-31-5

Designed and produced for The British
Horse Society and The Pony Club by
Threshold Books Limited
661 Fulham Road, London SW6 5PZ

Text by Elwyn Hartley Edwards
Consultant: Howard Cooper
Photographs by Kit Houghton
Line drawings by Carole Vincer
Designed by Alan Hamp

Typeset by Rapid Communications Ltd
London WC1

Printed and bound in Great Britain by
Hollen Street Press Ltd, Slough

Contents

1

The Evolution of the Horse

The Age of the Reptiles came to an end some 70 million years ago. The dinosaurs, pterodactyls, plesiosaurs and other giant lizards became extinct because of changes in climate, plant growth and terrain, to which they were unable to adapt.

With the dying out of the reptiles the Age of Mammals began, in the Eocene period of the Tertiary (third) era. Eocene means 'dawn period' and within it are to be found the ancestors of present-day mammals. (The starting point for our own ancestors occurs much later with a small tree-dwelling ape, *proconsul*, living in the forests of central Africa 25 million years ago in the Miocene period.) One of these Eocene creatures was a small round-backed animal which scientists have named *Eohippus*, the Dawn Horse, from which it has been possible to trace the development of the species to the modern members of the horse family, *Equus*.

This first 'horse' in no way resembled the present-day animal. From the remarkably complete skeletons discovered in North America, first in 1867 and then in 1932, palaeontologists at the California Institute of Technology were able to build a fairly accurate reconstruction of the Dawn Horse to reveal an animal weighing on average about 12 pounds (5.4 kg) and standing some 14 inches (35 cms) high at the shoulder. This is about the size of a fox or a middle-size dog.

In the context of this book, however, it is the feet which are of particular interest. The foot was multi-toed: four clawed toes on the forefeet and three behind. To the rear of the toes was a large pad similar to that of the dog and the tapir, an animal which is related to the horse species and which in many respects is considered to resemble the forerunners of the *equidae*.

This foot formation allowed *Eohippus* to cross without difficulty the wet, soft ground found at the edges of pools and streams in the jungle-type environment in which the animal lived. Part of the pad, which was an essential element in these conditions, persists vestigially as the ergot in the modern horse: that thick horny growth on the point of the fetlock. (The 'chestnuts', the warty growths on the inside of the fore and hind legs, are considered to have once been scent glands, a function now lost through disuse.)

In the process of animal evolution, environment is the greatest single factor, and as the earth's climate, terrain and vegetation changed imperceptibly over millions of years, the dentition, sight and method of locomotion employed by the horse's ancestors had to adapt to the new requirements.

Mesohippus and his close successor *Miohippus* came on to the scene in the Oligocene period 40-25 million years ago. These were bigger animals, possibly twice the size of *Eohippus*. Their teeth equipped them to browse efficiently on the greater variety of soft plant growth which had become available, and the altered ground conditions caused changes in the feet. Both fore and hind feet now had three toes, and increasingly the weight was borne on the central toe of the trio.

In the 50-odd million years between *Eohippus* and *Equus*, lush jungle-type vegetation gave way first to temperate-zone forest and then, 25 million years ago, in the Miocene period, to treeless grasslands and firm ground. By the mid-Pliocene period, about six million years ago, the final prototype for *Equus* was emerging. This was *Pliohippus* from which descends the true horse and also the zebras, asses and hermionids. The animal stood some 49 inches (124 cms) high at the wither, and the general proportions of his skull, body and limbs corresponded closely to those of the modern horse.

The outer toes had become atrophied 'splints' quite early in the Pliocene period, and they survive in the modern horse as the two small bones on either side of the cannon. Mid-way through that time, the animal was moving on a single toe, or hoof, not that much different from the foot with which we are familiar.

One million years ago the process was complete, and the species *Equus Caballus* was established on the earth as an herbivorous, herd animal equipped to survive the attack of predators, of which man was in time to become the most dangerous. In defence, the animal had developed a set of heightened senses, including all-round vision and the ability to flee swiftly away from danger, whether real or imagined, by virtue of long limbs terminating in a single ligament-sprung hoof. The latter had the characteristic covering of hard horn, and the major part of the original pad had become extended into the sole of the foot as the thick wedge-shaped piece of rubbery horn known as the *frog*, which acts as a non-slip and anti-concussive device.

For reasons which can only be matters of conjecture, the equine species became extinct in America, 'the cradle of the horse,' following the Ice Age, when that continent became isolated from Europe and Asia by the disappearance of the connecting land bridges.

It was not re-introduced until early in the 16th century, when the Spanish *conquistadores* imported horses to Cuba in readiness for their conquest of Mexico.

Domestication

The first animal to be 'domesticated' by man was the dog, the natural companion to man the hunter. Dogs seem to have found a place at the fireside around 12,000 BC. Three thousand years later, sheep were being kept by the pastoral people of the Middle East, and by 7,000 BC, as nomadic peoples began to settle into permanent communities, goats, pigs and cattle were all domesticated.

It is, however, the nomadic peoples of the Eurasian steppes

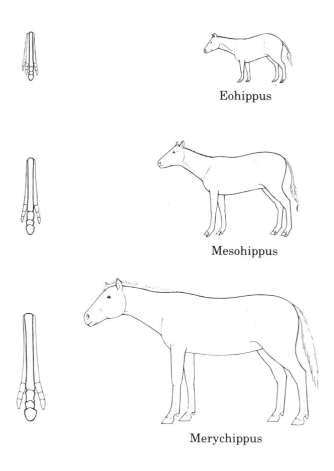

Eohippus

Mesohippus

Merychippus

Fig. 1   *The evolutionary process which began with the multi-toed*
Eohippus *(top left) in the Eocene Period 55 million years ago*
continued through Mesohippus *and* Merychippus *to the first*
single-toed animal Pliohippus *(top right), which developed during*

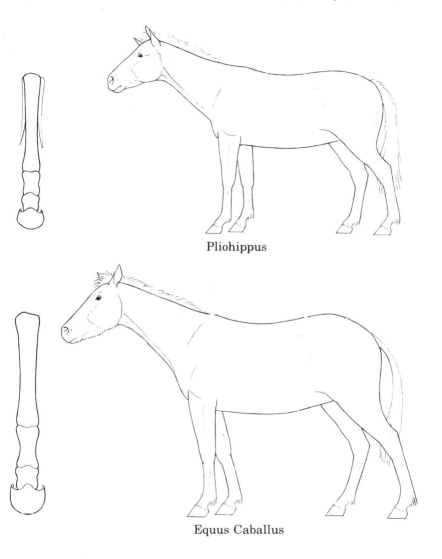

Pliohippus

Equus Caballus

the mid-Pliocene Period some six million years ago. A million years ago the process was completed and the species Equus Caballus *was established on the Earth.*

who are generally credited with the early domestication of the horse some 5-6,000 years ago, towards the end of the Neolithic period. They were probably Aryan tribes moving about the steppes bordering the Caspian and Black Seas. Initially, they herded horses – as they might previously have herded reindeer – obtaining milk and meat from their animals, as well as hides to be made into tents and dung to be used as fuel. They represented the first of the great horse cultures, and related tribes – notably the Kassites and Elamites – had conquered northwest Persia early in the second millenium BC. In the same period the Hyksos had ridden their ponies into Asia Minor, and a little later, using horse-drawn chariots, they were to penetrate into Egypt to create the Hittite Empire.

After them came a succession of peoples relying upon horse-power to create, expand and maintain their empires. Egyptians, Assyrians, Persians, all in time gave way to the classical civilisations of Greece and Rome, but it was not until the beginning of the Christian era that the practice of protecting the hoof with an iron shoe became general.

Development of the horseshoe

The Assyrians and the Hittites were skilled workers in iron. As a result of their conquests their expertise in this field spread first to Mesopotamia, then to Egypt and thence along the trade routes into Europe. By the year 600 BC the Celts and Gauls, who later formed the bulk of the Roman cavalry, were the foremost ironworkers of the ancient world. It is to them that the invention of the nailed horseshoe is attributed. They were established in Britain in 450 BC and it is possible that they were shoeing horses in this country before the Roman invasion of 55 BC.

Neither the Greeks, nor the Romans, before their contact with the 'barbarian' Celts and Gauls, used nailed horseshoes. However, they and the early horse-peoples did use a type of sandal, which they fitted on footsore animals. At first, they were made of woven grass and later of leather secured to the foot by thongs. The Roman *soleae* was a boot of this type, whilst the *soleae Sparteae*, revealing the Greek influence, was made from plaited grass or rope. Similar horse boots were used in Japan up to the 19th century.

Soleae ferreae (i.e. iron shoe) was the name given to the shoes made by the Celts and appears to have come into use in the early years of the Roman occupation of Britain.

The earliest form of metal shoe used by the Romans was the *hipposandal*, a plate with raised side pieces which was kept in place by thongs. Its use, however, would have been confined to veterinary cases since it would not have been practical as a working shoe.

The reason why the horse-peoples of the Middle East found it unnecessary to employ protective horseshoes was that they operated in dry conditions which are conducive to the formation of exceptionally strong hard-wearing horn.

In the wet conditions of Europe, on the other hand, the hooves become soft and are easily broken, quickly rendering the horse unfit for service. The extensive road systems created by the Romans, along with the damp atmosphere, also contributed to excessive wear of the hooves.

Although iron oxidises rapidly and disintegrates, making exact dating difficult, there are numerous examples of shoes of the *Romano-Gallic*, *Romano-British* periods, many of them recovered from burial mounds (the practice of burying horses with their owner is an ancient one and persisted well beyond the Christian era). The Celtic horseshoes were small (about 4½ ins or 11 cms wide) but were practical and of quite sophisticated workmanship.

The outline of the branches is wavy, due to the punching of round nail holes, which are countersunk. The foot surface is flat and the ground surface slightly concave. The nails of the period are short and round in the shank and the head has a characteristic 'violin-key' shape. Some shoes have the ends of the branches turned over to form a calkin, a device contributing to a better foothold which is still used today.

Shoes of this type were in evidence between 50 BC and

AD 50 but by the end of the Roman occupation refinements had been made and plain shoes with square nails were making their appearance. Otherwise little change occurred until the coming of the Normans in 1066. This marked the second period in the development of the horseshoe: the

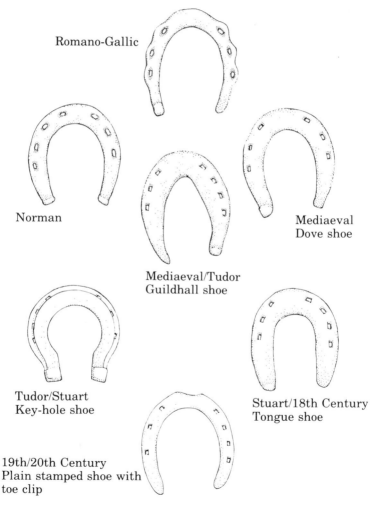

Romano-Gallic

Norman

Mediaeval
Dove shoe

Mediaeval/Tudor
Guildhall shoe

Tudor/Stuart
Key-hole shoe

Stuart/18th Century
Tongue shoe

19th/20th Century
Plain stamped shoe with
toe clip

Mediaeval or *Packhorse* period which extended from 1066 to around 1550.

The Normans, much concerned with the need to shoe their horses correctly, brought with them their 'farriers'. The French word is *ferrier*, derived from the Latin *ferrum*. Control of the Norman farriers was handed by William The Conqueror to Henry de *Farrariis* or de *Ferrars*, whose descendants became the Earls of Ferrers and bore six horseshoes on the quarterings of their coat-of-arms.

The distinguishing features of the shoes within this period are the absence of countersunk nail holes and the complete elimination of the wavy branch. Fullering of the shoe was not practised in Britain during the period but quantities of shoes imported from Flanders in the 15th century were of the fullered pattern. The practice must therefore have been general in parts of Europe before it found a wider acceptance during the Renaissance.

The most important advance in British farriery during the Mediaeval-Packhorse period was the formation of a 'Fellowship' in 1356 by the Mayor of the City of London as a result of 'many offences and dangers' committed by farriers within the City. The object was to exercise control over the standards of the craft, and this body, incorporated by Royal Charter in 1692, was the forerunner of the Worshipful Company of Farriers established that same year by the court of aldermen as a livery company.

The period from 1550 to 1800 is known as the *Renaissance* and *Key-Hole* period: key-hole because of the distinctive shape of some of the shoes produced. Clips were not yet

Fig. 2 Left: *The development of the horseshoe falls into four distinct periods: Romano-Gallic, Romano-British, characterised by the wavy outline of the branches (top); Mediaeval or Packhorse (1066-1550 AD), examples of which are illustrated by the three shoes in the second row; Renaissance and Key-hole (1550-1800 AD), of which the two shoes in the third row are typical; and the modern period beginning in the 19th century in which fullering was practised and clips introduced.*

employed, but fullering of the shoe was commonplace, and because of the volume of literature on the subject by the enquiring horsemen of this 'classical' period of equitation, shoes were made in great variety, many of them being surgical or remedial.

The establishment of veterinary schools in the 18th and 19th centuries (the 'modern' period is taken as being from 1800 onwards) gave added impetus to scientific studies of shoeing. Some were wide of the mark and resulted in harmful practices, in particular the excessive paring of the sole and frog and the rasping of the foot wall. These and other examples of mistaken practice persisted well into the 19th century, and it was a very long time before farriery became based on scientific principles of physiology and anatomy and it became accepted that the foot should be maintained in its natural state.

By the end of the 19th century, apart from a wide range of surgical shoes, the fullered shoe was well-established although, as is the case today, the plain stamped shoe was much in evidence. Nails were countersunk and clips were introduced to help hold the shoe securely in place and reduce the strain carried by the nails themselves as the foot strikes the ground.

2

The Foot – Function and Structure

The foot is a component part of the overall structure of the horse, and must be thought of as such when studying conformation and the practice of shoeing.

The leg muscles of a horse lie above the knee in the forelegs and above the hocks in the hind legs. The lower legs above the feet (and to which the feet are directly related) are made up of bones, ligaments, tendons and accompanying arteries and veins.

Locomotion

Movement in the structure is created by the contraction and extension of muscles (hence *flexor* and *extensor* muscles). The muscles move in pairs (i.e. *flexor/extensor*), activating joints through the connecting tendons. Muscle is made up of upper and lower parts. The upper, belly, part consists of red fibres and is capable of greater expansion and contraction than the lower part which is made up of the hard fibres of the tendon – (the *tendinous* portion).

A TENDON is a 'rope' made of a tough, elastic substance. At one end it is virtually plaited into the belly muscle whilst at the other it is fastened firmly to the bone.

A JOINT is made where two bones meet. The ends of the bones which form a joint – the articular surfaces – are of greater density than the rest of the bone, so as to withstand friction.

The Foot – Function and Structure

The two bone surfaces are further protected by layers of gristle, known as *cartilage*.

A membrane, the *joint capsule*, surrounds the joint in two layers. The outer layer is thick and acts as a support to the joint formation. The inner layer secretes a fluid (*synovia* or joint oil) which lubricates the joint, permitting it to operate within 'a bath of oil.'

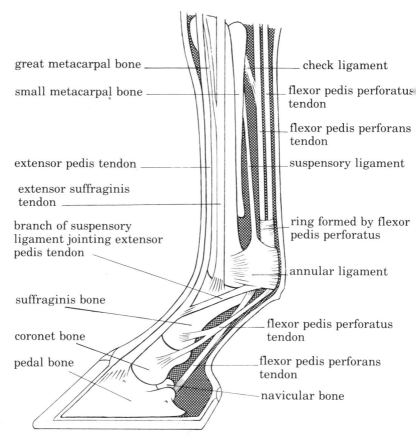

great metacarpal bone

small metacarpal bone

extensor pedis tendon

extensor suffraginis tendon

branch of suspensory ligament jointing extensor pedis tendon

suffraginis bone

coronet bone

pedal bone

check ligament

flexor pedis perforatus tendon

flexor pedis perforans tendon

suspensory ligament

ring formed by flexor pedis perforatus

annular ligament

flexor pedis perforatus tendon

flexor pedis perforans tendon

navicular bone

Fig. 3 *Ligaments and tendons of the lower leg.*

The whole skeleton is held together by *ligaments*, which as well as joining bone to bone, govern the movement of the joint, allowing it to move only as far as it is able. If the foot is out of balance in relation to the bones of the lower limb, or to the overall conformation, this may mean that the tendon is sprained or damaged. The action of the joint will then be impaired to a greater or lesser extent.

The Foot

The term FOOT is used to describe the hoof, the horny covering, and all the structures that it contains. The construction of a well-formed foot allows it to:
(a) resist wear; (b) support the weight of the horse; (c) limit concussion (caused by striking the ground) and thus reduce the jarring effect throughout the lower leg; (d) prevent slipping. For convenience the foot can be examined in two parts – the outer, non-vascular INSENSITIVE FOOT and the INNER SENSITIVE FOOT.

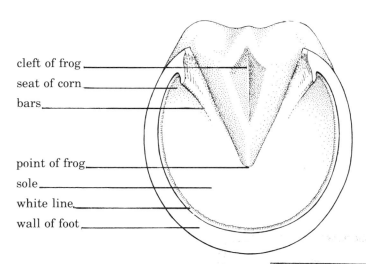

cleft of frog
seat of corn
bars

point of frog
sole
white line
wall of foot

Fig. 4 *Bearing surface of the foot.*

THE INSENSITIVE FOOT consists of the WALL, the SOLE and the FROG.

The wall is made of dense horn. It is divided into the *toe* – i.e. the portion at the front of the foot – and the *quarters* at the sides, which in turn pass into the *heels*. The horn is thickest at the toe and narrows towards the quarters and heels.

The wall does not encircle the hoof. It turns inwards at the heels to form the BARS which are joined to both the frog and the sole.

As the bars are part of the wall, they take a proportion of the weight and provide more bearing surface and greater strength at the heels. The circle of the hard wall is not complete, so the bars allow for the foot to expand as it meets the ground, thus helping to prevent it from being jarred.

The area of the sole between the wall and the bars is known as the *seat of corn*. Corns are caused by undue pressure from poorly shaped feet and from shoes that are ill-fitting or left on for too long.

The bars must be left to grow normally. If they are cut away, the support provided by the heels is removed and the foot becomes contracted and unable to expand.

The *external surface* of the wall is convex, sloping obliquely downwards. The slope is less apparent at the quarters than at the toe and is far more apparent at the heels. The rings discernible on the hoof indicate variations in the *growth rate* of the wall.

As with a human nail, the horn grows continually and varies in thickness and rate of growth. On average, newly formed horn at the coronet takes nine months to reach ground level. The growth rate per month can thus be estimated at between ¼ to ⅜ inch (6 to 10 mm) and in some instances will be in excess of that figure.

The *colour* of the hoof is governed by the colour of the skin at the coronet. White skin, which is devoid of pigment, is accompanied by white horn which some experts consider to be softer than the blue/black hoof colour.

The *periople* is the rim of soft horn at the junction of the hoof with the coronary band. It extends over the wall like a membrane, and is thicker on the upper part. Its function is to provide a protective film controlling evaporation.

Continual rasping of the wall causes excessive evaporation of the natural foot moisture (approximately 25 per cent), and the feet become brittle. Conversely, if the normal evaporation rate is halted – as it may be by the application of impervious dressings such as varnishes and polish – fluid will accumulate and the horn will be softened.

On the inside of the wall are layers of horny, *insensitive laminae* which dovetail into the layers of fleshy, *sensitive leaves* of the inner sensitive foot.

The position of the horny laminae is marked by the *white line*. This is soft, plastic horn which runs round the inside of the wall and is easily seen on the scrubbed sole of an unshod foot. It indicates to the farrier the thickness of the wall and

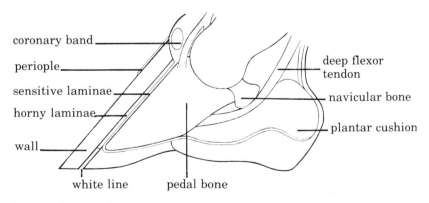

Fig. 5 *Section through centre of foot.*

allows him accurately to assess the angle ('pitch') at which to drive the nails so that they give a good hold without risk of either 'binding' or 'pricking' the foot. (Binding occurs if the nail is too close to the sensitive laminae and presses upon it when the foot takes the weight. Pricking occurs when the nail actually penetrates the sensitive structure.)

The *white line*, as well as joining the wall to the sole, allows a little 'give' in the sole when weight is put on the foot.

The sole forms the ground surface of the foot. The thick outer, insensitive part is covered with flakes of protective horn which if pared away (for the sake of appearance) weakens the natural 'arch' and reduces the protective thickness.

A healthy sole is firm and thick. It is also noticeably concave – particularly in the hind feet.

The *function* of the sole is to protect the sensitive structures above it whilst supporting weight around its outer edge. The concavity of the sole allows it to *support* weight but is not in itself a weight-bearing surface.

The frog is the v-shaped structure of soft, elastic horn lying between the bars of the foot. An important anti-concussion mechanism, it bears some degree of the animal's weight, and its wedge shape provides a good non-slip foothold. The pliable quality of the frog is due to its fluid content (about 40 per cent) which is higher than in any other part of the foot.

When the foot comes to the ground the compression of the frog causes it to expand. At the same time it is pushed upwards against the *digital cushion* which is situated between it and the under surface of the pedal bone. This in turn expands, absorbing and reducing concussion and itself bringing pressure through the *lateral cartilages* on to the wall, which has then to follow suit with a similar expansion.

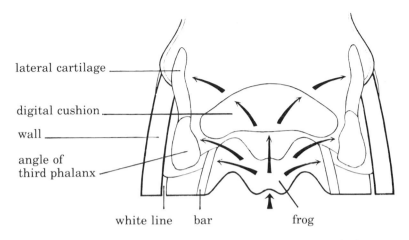

lateral cartilage

digital cushion

wall

angle of
third phalanx

white line   bar   frog

Fig. 6   *Cross-section of the foot from the rear showing how the foot*
expands as the weight causes the frog to be compressed.

For the frog to fulfil its purpose and to remain healthy,
it must come into ground contact. If it is prevented from
so doing it atrophies, the heels close, and the foot becomes
contracted. This has a serious effect on the circulation of
blood and can cause the foot to become diseased. The
increase in concussion may lead to problems throughout the
lower limbs.

Maintaining the frog as nearly as possible in its natural
state is a major requirement in the preparation and shoeing
of a foot. When a shoe is fitted to a foot, thus raising the wall
half an inch or 13 mm from the ground, the function of the
frog is inevitably more restricted when the horse is working
on road surfaces. However, on soft, cross-country going, the
frog in a shod foot will function to its full extent.

THE INNER SENSITIVE FOOT, which contains blood
vessels, provides nutrition to the hoof. Within its insensitive
protective casing it houses: (1) the *third phalanx: pedal* or

coffin bone, (2) the *second phalanx:* the short pastern or coronet bone, which is jointed to the third phalanx; (3) the *navicular* bone which is situated at the back of the pedal bone; and (4) the *lateral cartilages.* These stem from the wings of the pedal bone. They function as shock absorbers for the sensitive foot, and contain and support the digital cushion.

The *lateral cartilages* are large and can easily be felt above the coronet. They allow a degree of elasticity in the rear part of the foot, but they can become less elastic with age. If they eventually are ossified, the condition is known as 'sidebone', which can be relieved by corrective shoeing.

The *sensitive sole* supplies nutrition to the horny sole. The *sensitive frog* provides nourishment for the important *digital cushion* with which it is merged.

Because of its ability to expand, the *digital cushion*, which at its posterior base is divided by the *bulbs of the heel*, plays an important part in reducing concussion. It is also closely concerned with the *circulation of blood*. The blood supply within the foot is considerable, and plays a large part in absorbing the pressures to which the structure is constantly subjected. The bones and sensitive parts within the hoof are held in a virtual state of buoyancy by its presence.

Once it has fed the tissues of the leg and foot, the blood, pumped through the arteries, becomes de-oxygenated. It is then received into the digital cushion. As the frog is compressed by contact with the ground the pressure is transmitted to the cushion, and on its return journey to the heart its blood content is forced upwards through the veins.

Conformation

The word conformation relates to the shape and form of the horse and depends on the length of the bones, their proportionate relationship, and the angles they make with each other.

Conformation governs the position of the centre of gravity and the horse's athletic potential. Correct proportions and overall balance in the structure ensure that the lateral parts of the limbs bear weight evenly and equally and that the movement is 'straight': i.e. that the limbs are moved directly to their front without deviation, the hind legs following exactly the track of the forelimbs.

It is not possible to alter conformational defects in the limbs, but they can be improved and alleviated by corrective shoeing if it is undertaken early enough in the horse's life.

Foreleg

When the horse is standing squarely, the weight is distributed in the ratio 60 to 40 per cent between the fore and hind legs. This to an extent accounts for the difference in shape between the front and rear feet.

Viewed from the front, both forelegs should be straight and parallel, the feet slightly separated. A vertical line dropped from the point of the shoulder should divide the limb into two equal parts, the line passing through the centre of the knee and the foot (see *Fig. 7* page 24). Front and hind limbs should be in exact alignment.

Viewed from the side, a vertical line dropped from the centre of the forearm at its juncture with the trunk should again divide the limb equally, passing centrally through knee and fetlock and meeting the ground just behind the heels.

Variations on this ideal conformation place undue strain on the limb's component parts; as follows:

NARROW BASE. A reduction in the width of the base, caused by the feet being too close, and often resulting in a pigeon-toed stance, places uneven wear on the joints. This

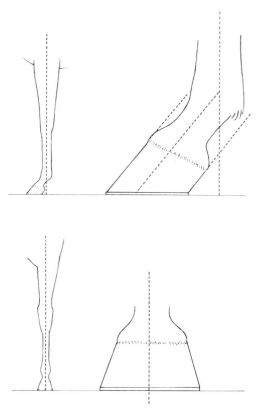

Fig. 7   *Side and front views of a normal limb and foot.*

can give rise to osteoarthritis, sidebones, and articular windgalls. Pigeon toes – which occur most frequently in broad-chested horses – cause excessive wear on the outside of the feet.

WIDE BASE. When the feet are placed so far apart that a vertical line falls inside the hooves, uneven wear occurs on the opposite side of the joints. The toes are frequently turned out and greater wear is sustained on the inside of the feet. The same diseases as those mentioned above may occur.

If the knees are turned outwards, considerable stress is placed on the lower leg ligaments. This also happens when

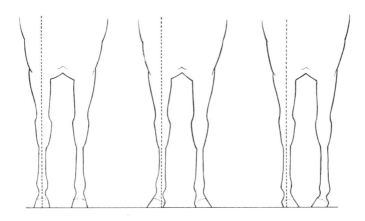

Fig. 8 *Normal front limbs; turned-out toes combined with a wide base formation; narrow base formation with turned-in toes.*

the knees are turned in opposite fashion: i.e. knock knees.
CALF KNEE is a term applied to a leg curving inward below the knee. It is a serious conformational fault which causes strains on the check ligament and excessive strain on the components of the knee joint.
TIED-IN BELOW THE KNEE describes a foreleg in which the measurement around the cannon below the knee is significantly less than a measurement taken lower down nearer the fetlock joint. It constricts the passage of the tendons and usually results in unsoundness.

Hind Leg

From the rear, a line drawn from the point of the buttock should pass through the centre of the hock, fetlock and foot. From the side, a line from the point of the buttock to the ground should touch the point of the hock and then coincide with the vertical line formed by the rear of the cannon bone. Anything inside or outside this line may lead to stress and possible disease in the hock. *Sickle hocks* strain the rear of

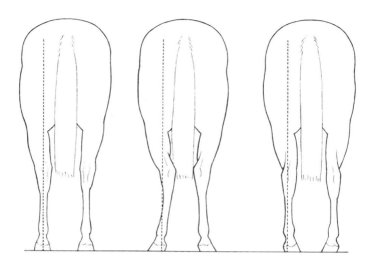

Fig. 9 Left to right: *Normal hind limbs; wide base formation of the hind limbs; narrow base formation. The toe out, wide base contributes to cow hocks, the opposite to bowed hocks.*

the hock joint and can result in a sprain of the plantar ligament which will cause a 'curb'. Other faults are:

NARROW BASE. A conformation in which the feet are placed too close together, the hocks being bowed outwards. Much uneven stress is put on the lateral aspects of the limb.

WIDE BASE. Caused by 'cow hocks,' the points being carried too close. The hock joint is particularly affected and the conformation is associated with bone spavin.

Foot-Pastern Axis (FPA)

The exactly even articulation of the cannon bone (*metacarpal*) and the first phalanx (*suffraginis* or *long pastern*), the second phalanx (*coronet bone* or *short pastern*) and the third phalanx (*pedal* or *coffin bone*) depends upon an axis which relates closely to that of the shoulder. It produces specific angles at the fetlock, toe and heel and thus ensures the least concussive and most economical flight path for the foot.

The ideal inclination of a good riding shoulder from the highest point of the wither to the point of the shoulder is generally accepted as being 43–45 degrees, and the ideal FPA should approximate very closely to that figure.

When viewed from the front the pastern axis is an imaginary straight line from the centre of the fetlock through the pastern joint and foot, creating an equal division between the two. Viewed from the side, the imaginary line begins in the centre of the fetlock and divides into two equal parts the pastern joint joining the first and second phalanges. The foot axis extends from the coronary band to the point where the

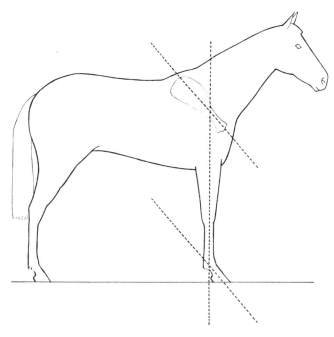

Fig. 10 *The ideal foot-pastern axis (FPA) should approximate to the slope of the shoulder.*

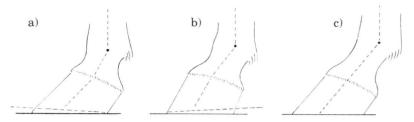

Fig. 11 · *Abnormal FPA caused by a) too long a toe resulting in the FPA being broken back; b) foot too high at the heel so that the FPA is broken forward; c) normal FPA achieved by correcting the growth at toe or heel.*

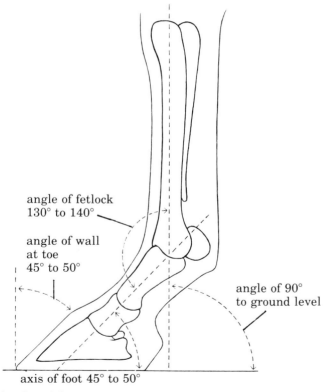

angle of fetlock
130° to 140°

angle of wall
at toe
45° to 50°

angle of 90°
to ground level

axis of foot 45° to 50°

Fig. 12 *Angles of the joints in normal FPA.*

foot meets the ground and is parallel with the preferred angle of the forefoot, 50 degrees.

The FPA in the hind feet is slightly steeper, by about 5 degrees.

When the foot-pastern axis is correct, the legs are moved in alignment with the body, the toe being pointed forward.

Departures from the ideal FPA are caused either by conformational differences and/or failings, or by an excessive growth at the toe or heel which is not corrected in the preparation of the foot. Too much growth at the toe causes the axis to be broken to the rear whilst an opposite excess causes the axis line to be broken forwards. Both can be corrected – by lowering the toe in the first instance or the heel in the second.

There are, however, horses with a naturally long pastern and sloping foot or with a naturally upright foot. Both will still retain a straight FPA, and to attempt to rasp feet of this sort would only result in breaking the axis line unnecessarily.

Faulty conformation is usually made evident in the action, as in the case of toes turning in or out. If they turn *in*, the FPA is inclined obliquely inwards, if they turn *out* it is inclined outwards. With toes turning in there is exaggerated wear of the outside wall, and vice-versa when the toes turn out.

NORMAL FEET

The normal forefoot is rounded at the toe, with the wall curving more on the outside than the inside. The slope of the outer quarter is always greater than that of the inner. The angle of the wall is between 45 and 50 degrees.

The hind foot is oval at the toe. The sole is more concave than in the forefoot, the frog is smaller, and both inner and outer quarters more upright. The angle of the wall is between 50 and 55 degrees.

ABNORMAL FEET

These are due to a defect in the foot itself and are not concerned with any failing in the conformation of the limb.

UPRIGHT FEET are high at the heels and short at the toe with the angle of the wall in excess of 50 degrees in front and 55 degrees behind.

SLOPED FEET are those less than 45 degrees in front or 55 degrees in the hind feet.

CLUB OR MULE FEET. This is an example of an accentuated upright foot with the angle of the wall above 60 and 65 degrees in fore and hind feet respectively.

FLAT FEET are those in which the soles lack the usual concavity. They are prone to becoming bruised in consequence.

DROPPED SOLE. The sole, having collapsed forms a convex shape which extends below the surface of the wall. It occurs in cases of chronic laminitis.

THIN SOLE. Such soles are easily bruised, in spite of being concave in shape. Usually they are accompanied by thin walls.

BRITTLE FEET. These are usually caused by loss of moisture from the hoof, and sometimes occur in spells of very dry weather. They result in shoeing problems, as they split easily when nailed. A remedy is to soak the feet in water, or to apply oil which limits the evaporation.

GAIT

NORMAL ACTION. The foot breaks over at the toe, with the flight of the foot reaching the apex of the arc as it passes the opposite leg.

With a sloping FPA the break-over is delayed, reaching the peak of the arc *before* passing the opposite leg. The stride tends to be longer and lower and the ride is comfortable.

When the axis is upright the foot breaks over quickly, reaching the apex of the flight arc *after* it has passed the opposite leg.

The stride is reduced and the concussion increased by the sharp angle at which the foot meets the ground. The ride is uncomfortable.

Abnormalities occur as a direct result of a conformational defect.

PADDLING OR DISHING is when the foot is swung in an outward arc. It causes wear on the outside quarter. Horses with toe-in conformation display this failing.

WINGING is a more serious failing since it causes the horse to brush one foot against the other. It occurs in horses with toe-out conformation. The foot is swung in an inward circle, and wear occurs on the inside quarter.

PLAITING. In simple terms, the horse crosses his forelegs,

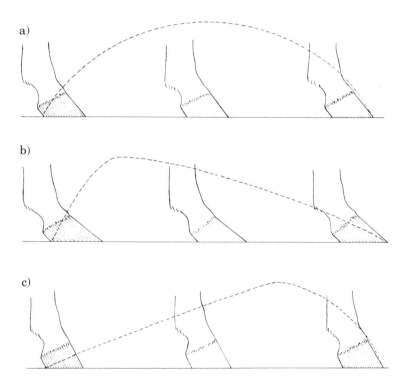

a)

b)

c)

Fig. 13 *Flight of the foot with a) normal FPA; b) sloping FPA and c) upright.*

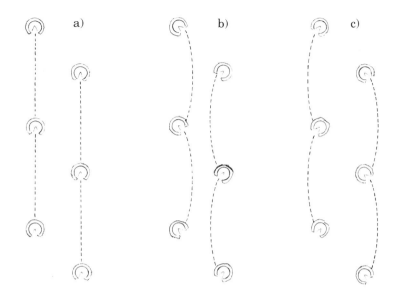

Fig. 14 *Flight of the forefeet: a) normal; b) toe-out conformation; c) toes turned in.*

which in extreme cases causes serious stumbling. It is confined to horses with a toe-out, narrow base conformation.

Defects of toe-in, toe-out and foot-pastern axis cause abnormal wear of the shoe.

The state of wear in the shoe provides a lot of information, so shoes should be studied before the foot is prepared and the type of shoe selected.

Lameness

The most suitable pace at which to detect lameness is the trot, in which the support for the lame leg will be restricted to its diagonal partner. The horse should be run out on a firm, level surface on a loose rein which does not interfere with the carriage of the head.

LAMENESS IN FRONT is more easily discerned when the horse is trotted towards you. When the lame leg touches the ground, the head is raised in an effort to relieve the pain. When the sound leg comes down, the horse 'nods' or drops his head.

LAMENESS BEHIND can best be seen as the horse is trotted away. The quarter on the lame side is raised as the lame foot takes the weight, and the quarter is lowered when the sound foot touches the ground.

Lameness in both front feet produces a stiff, much restricted movement, with the horse being unwilling to lift the feet well clear of the ground. Lameness in both hind legs causes a much shortened stride and an unsteady gait. The horse will have obvious difficulty in backing.

3

The Horseshoe

PARTS OF THE SHOE

The shoe comprises the *toe, quarters, heels* and *branches*. The *branch* is from the *toe* to the *heel* on each side.

☐ The area of the shoe covered by the TOE is between the first nail holes on each side. The QUARTER lies between the last nail hole and the heel.

The *web* refers to the width and depth of the metal. The width is known as the *cover* (e.g. a wide-webbed shoe would be said to give '*plenty of cover*').

☐ The two surfaces of the shoe are the *foot surface*, meeting the bearing surface of the foot, and the *ground surface*.

☐ A *set* consists of four shoes: a *pair* of front shoes and a *pair* of hind shoes.

☐ The most common materials for riding-horse shoes are *concave fullered steel* and *flat iron bar*. Aluminium is used for racehorse shoes. Farriers can buy both from the steel mill in different weights, the former being fullered ready to be made up at the forge.

SHOE SIZES

Generally, fullered steel is available in four widths from ½ inch (13 mm) to ⅞ inch (22 mm) and in various thicknesses. Flat iron bar is usually made in two widths: ⅞ inch (22 mm) and 1 inch (25 mm). Machine-made shoes, other than racing plates, are of three types: plain stamped, three-quarter fullered and concave fullered. They are available in the following sizes:

Plain stamped in ½ inch (13 mm) shoe widths (measured

across broadest part of shoe) from 4 to 7½ inches (10 to 19 cms).

Three-quarter fullered ½ inch (13 mm) sizes from 4 to 7 inches (10 to 18 cms).

Concave fullered ½ inch (13 mm) sizes from 3½ to 6 inches (9 to 15 cms).

□ Concave steel is wider on the foot surface than on the ground surface. Together with the grooving (fullering) this allows for a lighter shoe which improves the foothold, prevents slipping on tarmac, and reduces the effects of suction in heavy going.

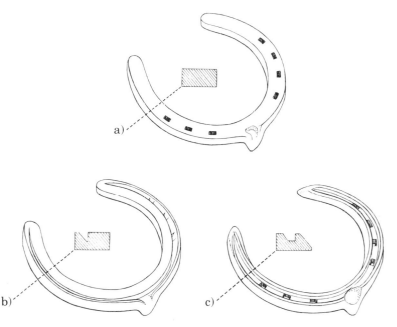

Fig. 15 *Types of horseshoe: (a) plain stamped shoe, (b) three-quarter fullered shoe; (c) concave fullered shoe.*

TYPES OF SHOE
Heavy horses or horses doing a lot of roadwork are often shod with *plain stamped shoes*. These have a level ground surface,

broken only by the nail holes, and wear better. Alternatively, a *three-quarter fullered shoe* may be used; because of the greater ground-bearing surface they are considered to be more durable than the full fullered shoe. Patterns other than these are occasionally used to counteract specific problems.

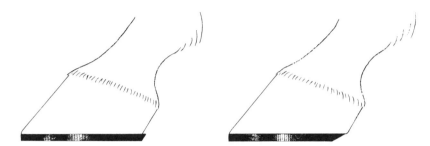

Fig. 16 *The heels of the front shoes should extend a little behind the bearing surface of the foot and be bevelled off at the same angle as the heel. For galloping, the shoes should end short of the bearing surface and be bevelled off obliquely.*

A *seated-out* shoe has the inner edge sloped to relieve pressure on the border of the sole. It can be beneficial in the case of flat feet, but the disadvantages are that it can be more easily pulled off by suction in deep going; also, dirt and grit can become lodged between the shoe and the foot. A *convex shoe* is sometimes fitted on horses who wear out their shoes very quickly. The inner edge of the ground surface of a convex shoe is thicker than the outer edge. This causes the inner edge to be worn first before the surface becomes level.

CLIPS

A clip is a triangular piece of metal, low and broad, drawn from the outer edge of the shoe and turned to lie flat on the hoof wall. Front shoes are fitted with a single 'toe' clip and hind ones have two 'quarter' clips, one on each side.

Toe clips hold the shoe in place while the nails are driven in, and thus help to ensure accurate fit. Quarter clips prevent the shoe from shifting sideways and allow the hind toe to be bevelled, reducing the risk of over-reaching.

A *rolled toe* on a shoe is a form of clip. It is used on horses who rapidly wear out the toe of a shoe, possibly by dragging a foot or even by continual pawing on the stable floor. To make it, the farrier turns the entire thickness of the toe portion upward, at an angle to the body of the shoe.

WEIGHT-WEAR
Heavy shoes encourage a horse to raise his feet in a high action. Light shoes act conversely, producing a long, low stride. For a riding horse, the lighter the shoe the better: though its wearing properties must be borne in mind. A shoe that is too light will need frequent replacement and the wall will suffer from constant nailing. A shoe that is too heavy increases the effort which has to be made with each stride. It is therefore unnecessarily fatiguing and puts extra stress on the limbs.

Shoes which are too thick raise the foot from the ground and prevent the frog from functioning; also, extra-long nails will be needed if the shoe is to be fitted securely.

The *wear* of a shoe depends upon so many factors that it is impossible to assess it accurately. On average it is estimated that a set of shoes lasts from four to five weeks. In any case, after that length of time the shoes have to be removed because of the growth of the horn, which must be levelled off. (When the old shoes are serviceable enough to be replaced, the operation is called a 'remove'.)

Horses with normal, straight action wear shoes evenly, with the exception of the outside of the toe, which will always become more worn than the rest of the shoe. Hind shoes wear out sooner than front shoes.

Where a horse wears out shoes very quickly he should be shod either with a convex or a wide web shoe, not with a heavier one.

NAILS

The number of nails used in securing the shoe should be 'as few as possible'.

☐ In practice, riding-horse shoes usually have seven nails: three on the inner branch and four on the outer. A pony shoe would require no more than five: three on the outside and two on the inner branch. Heavy working horses will need as many as nine. (The outside wall is slightly thicker than the inside, and the outer edge of the foot receives more wear.) Too many nail holes, placed close together, weaken the shoe.

☐ Modern nails are made from mild steel, in sizes from 2 (1⅝ inches or 41 mm in length) to 12 (2⅞ inches or 72 mm long): the size chosen depending on the nail hole and condition of the foot.

There are two faces to the nail, the outer one being straight. The point is bevelled so that it is forced towards the straight side when driven. The nail must always be driven with the outer face to the outside. The point will then be turned away from the sensitive structure and come through on the outside of the wall.

CALKINS – STUDS

Calkins are formed by turning over the heel of the shoe or welding a piece of steel to them. They increase the foothold on soft ground, but because they throw the foot on to the toe they are not suitable for tarmac roads.

When riding-horses are shod in this way the calkins are on the outside heels of the hind shoes. *Wedge* heels are used instead of the inside calkins to prevent brushing and to balance the feet.

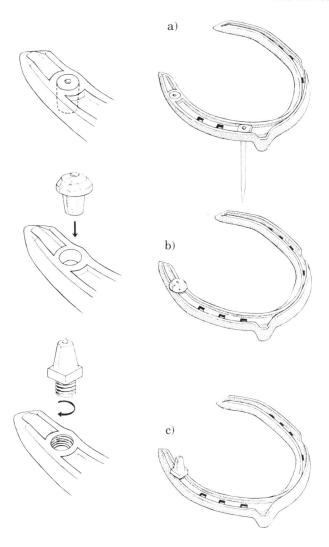

Fig. 17   *Studs: (a) countersunk road stud, only the projecting carbon tip comes into contact with the ground, and a tungsten-tipped road nail, (b) a tapered stud set permanently into the outside heel of the shoe, (c) screw-in stud fitted into a prepared, threaded hole.*

STUDS are available in a number of shapes and sizes suitable for a variety of purposes and ground conditions. They are more satisfactory than calkins.

For general use involving road work, standard, tapered studs can be set permanently into the heels of the shoes. As they are low and broad they do not interfere with the balance of the feet. In cases where balance might be affected, plug type studs can be countersunk into the shoes, so that only the projecting tip of tungsten carbide comes into contact with the ground.

Both types of stud have tips of tungsten, which is exceptionally hard-wearing and affords excellent grip on road surfaces. Road studs substantially increase the life of the shoes.

It is usual to fit studs of these patterns into the heels on both sides of the shoe. Though sometimes they are fitted to the hind shoes only, they can also be fitted to the front shoes.

SCREW-IN STUDS. For sporting activities these studs, fitted into prepared, threaded holes in the shoe, are preferable. For deep going large studs are generally used, whilst on hard ground H-shaped studs are advisable.

It is usual for screw-in studs to be fitted to the heels on the outside of the hind feet. (They may be used in conjunction with small road-type studs set into both heels of the forefeet.)

When the studs are not in use, the holes in the shoe must be plugged with tow. To fit the studs the plug is removed, the thread cleared with a screw tap ('tee-tap'), and the stud secured with a spanner.

It is not advisable to travel horses with the studs in position because of the risk of injury. They should be fitted immediately before the competition.

HORSESHOE BORIUM

The application of horseshoe borium (tungsten carbide

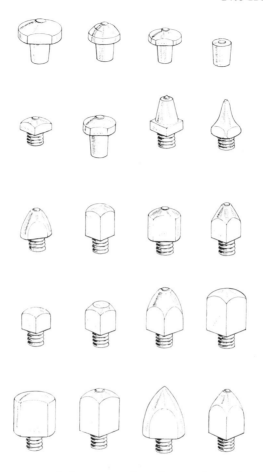

Fig. 18   *A variety of plug, tapered and screw-in studs.*

crystals packed in a tube of steel) gives shoes a rough, non-slip surface and considerably prolongs their life. However, because borium is expensive, it encourages the temptation to leave the shoes on too long, causing the nail holes to become enlarged and resulting in split hooves and loose shoes.

4

Principles and Methods of Shoeing

THE PURPOSE OF SHOEING

When horses are in work, particularly on hard or rough surfaces, the hoof is worn away more quickly than it can be replaced by natural growth. If the process were to be continued, the sensitive structures would be exposed, causing pain and lameness. The fitting of a shoe therefore *protects* the foot against injury, whilst improving its gripping properties.

The further objectives of the farrier are to maintain, to improve, and, where necessary, to correct:
□ The natural function of the foot.
□ The horse's natural action.
□ Conformational defects and faulty movement.
□ The effects of disease.

The well-shod horse whose foot structure is maintained at a high functional level and whose limbs are in as near perfect alignment as possible remains sound under a variety of conditions. His working life is extended and he can be expected to produce consistently high levels of performance.

THE FARRIER'S TOOLS

These fall into two groups: (1) *shoeing tools* used for preparing the foot and nailing the shoe and (2) *forge tools* used at the fire and anvil to make and shape the shoe.

Shoeing tools

HAMMER For shoeing, driving or nailing-on. It is light,

weighing 10-16 ounces (280-450 grammes). It has a large driving face and a short curved claw for bending and wringing off the nail ends where they emerge from the hoof.

BUFFER. A steel tool about 6 inches (15 cms) long. It has a chisel-shaped blade for cutting off 'clenches' and a point at the other end for punching broken nails and for cleaning nail holes.

PINCERS. Used for raising and levering off the shoe, for drawing nails, and for turning clenches. The jaws are kept sharp.

HOOF CUTTER. Similar to pincers but with one flat jaw and one sharp one. Used for cutting back the hoof wall. (A 'hoof

Fig. 19 *Shoeing tools.* Top *(left to right): toe knife, drawing knife, buffer.* Below: *hammer, clenching tongs, pincers and hoof cutter.* Bottom: *rasp.*

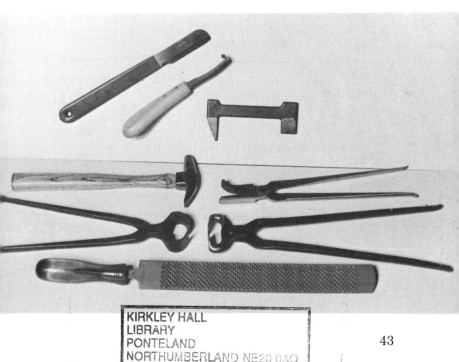

nipper', which has two sharp jaws, is favoured by some farriers.)

TOE KNIFE. This tool, often made from an old rasp, has a sharpened blade at the end. It is struck with a mallet to cut off overgrown hoof walls. It is a useful tool but requires skilful handling, as a slip could damage the foot.

DRAWING KNIFE. This has a curved blade, with the point turned over towards the inside. It can be used for lowering the wall, trimming, etc. The blunt edge is used for cleaning out the sole and the clefts of the frog.

SEARCHER. Similar to a drawing knife. Its purpose is to 'search' the foot for small stones, wounds etc.; to pare the horn around punctures; and to cut out corns.

RASP. A large file, one side coarse the other fine. The coarse surface removes unwanted wall, levels the bearing surface of the foot, and is used to finish off clenches. The fine surface is used for finishing off the shoe and for shaping clenches.

CLENCHING TONGS. A tool for pulling down the clenches. Particularly useful when shoeing young or difficult horses who may resent the use of the hammer.

Forge tools

ANVIL. The traditional anvil has a square body with a rounded 'beak' used for 'turning' and shaping the shoes. The working surface is used for welding and drawing iron.

At the 'heel' of the anvil there are two holes: one square (to take the shank of the 'tool', a mould through which the hot bar is pulled in order to give the required concave shape for the shoe), the other round. This latter is used to take the point of a punch or drift when making holes in the branch of the shoe.

FIRE TONGS. A long-handled tool with which the farrier can work hot metal without getting too close to the fire.

SHOE TONGS. Shorter than fire tongs, these are used for working the shoe on the anvil.

TURNING HAMMER. This type of hammer weighs between 2½ and 4 lbs, (1.1 and 1.8 kg) and has one flat and one convex face. It is used for forging, bending, and making clips.

SLEDGE HAMMER. A heavy hammer used for welding hot metal and hammering it through the 'tool' (see *Swage-Concave Tool* below).

STAMP. This is a punch used for making nail holes. It is shaped to the exact size of the nail head.

FULLER. A blunt chisel used for making the groove in the ground surface of the shoe: i.e. fullering.

SWAGE-CONCAVE TOOL, often known as 'the tool'. A mould through which the hot bar is drawn to make the concave shape. It is not in general use, as farriers can now buy steel which has already been fullered and made into the concave shape. It may be used if a heavier or wider shoe, outside the

Fig. 20 *Forge tools. Top (left to right): drift, punch, pritchel.* Below: *stamp, fire tongs, fuller, sledge hammer, turning hammer, swage or concave tool and heel cutter or half-round.*

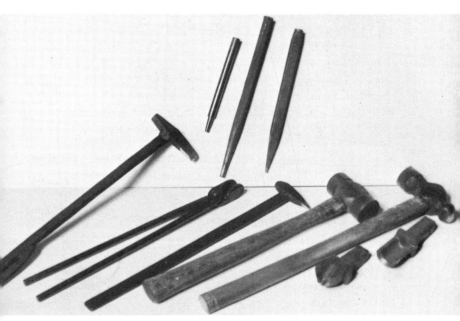

available metal range, is needed. The farrier will then make the special shoe from a length of plain bar metal.

PRITCHEL. A long steel punch. The end is shaped like the head of the nails used. The pritchel is used for carrying a hot shoe to the foot for fitting and for finishing off the nail holes punched by the stamp.

PUNCH AND DRIFT. The round punch is used for making stud holes. The drift, shaped to the exact size of the stud, is driven in to ensure a correct fit if a permanent stud is used.

TRIPOD-FOOTSTAND. A three-legged stand on which the foot is rested when it is brought forward to be finished off. Not now in common use but essential for shoeing heavy horses whose weight is too much to be held comfortably.

HOT AND COLD SHOEING

In HOT SHOEING the shoe is applied at dull red heat to the bearing surface of the foot before being cooled. It is then nailed on in the usual way. The charring of the horn shows the regularity or otherwise of the contact between the surface and the shoe. Any unevenness can be corrected with either knife or rasp, and the fit of the shoe can be altered on the anvil if necessary.

The charring of the horn also causes it to soften and expand because of the reduction made in the absorption of moisture. This allows the nails to be driven in more easily and to be more firmly secured when the horn contracts.

As horn is not a good conductor of heat, no pain is caused to the horse by the hot metal. However, the shoe should not be held to the foot longer than is absolutely necessary.

A bad workman could abuse the method by applying the shoe until it beds into the horn, to compensate for an unevenness in the fit. This could result in the sole itself being burned, so that the foot is made sore and the horse lame.

Fig. 21 Right: *Hot shoeing. Holding the hot shoe with the pritchel the farrier applies the shoe to the bearing surface of the foot.*

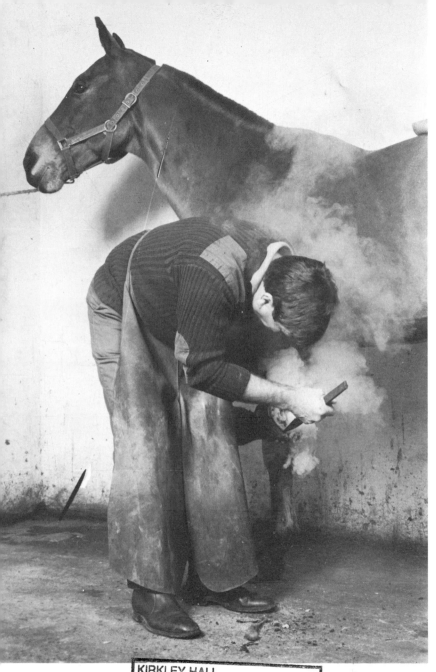

47

COLD SHOEING is often employed with machine-made shoes, which have a consistently level surface. Shoes can also be made in the forge to be brought to the horse and nailed on cold: but there can be only minor alterations to the outline of the shoe and none to the foot-bearing surface.

As an exact fit between shoe and foot is not possible, when cold shoeing, eventually the nails may be loosened, causing the clenches to rise. Hot shoeing is therefore preferable because it ensures a more accurate fit.

REMOVING THE SHOE

As a prelude to the shoe being removed, the foot has to be *picked up*. In the interests of safety it is advisable to follow the correct procedure.

□ *To pick up a foreleg*, stand at the horse's shoulder, facing the rear. Run your inside hand firmly and steadily down the back of the leg. Grip the pastern and then raise the foot. To place the horse's foot between your knees, take a step forward with your inside leg. Bring the foot under your knee and grip it with both hands. Then bend your knees and bring them together, with your toes turned in, so as to hold the foot firmly.

□ *To pick up a hind foot*, take up a position close to the horse's flank, facing the rear. Run your inside hand across the quarter and down the back of the leg to just above the fetlock joint. Raise the leg by pulling it towards you. When the leg is clear of the ground, take a step forward and cup the outside hand round the hoof wall. Another forward step with the inside leg allows the horse's lower leg to be placed across the handler's thigh, with the foot resting on the opposite knee.

To remove the shoe the buffer is used to cut off the clenches. With the pincers the shoe is then eased loose from the foot, first at the heels and then along each of the branches. The toe is then grasped and the shoe is pulled off backwards across the foot.

It is necessary for the clenches to be cut off cleanly so that

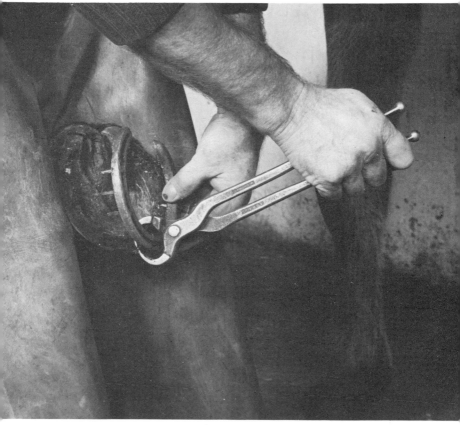

Fig. 22   *After the buffer has been used to cut off the clenches and the shoe eased from the foot, the shoe is pulled off backwards from the toe.*

nothing can damage the foot as the nails are pulled through the horn.

PREPARATION OF THE FOOT
When the shoe is removed, as much horn as has grown since the last shoeing is rasped off. To assess how much of the wall

49

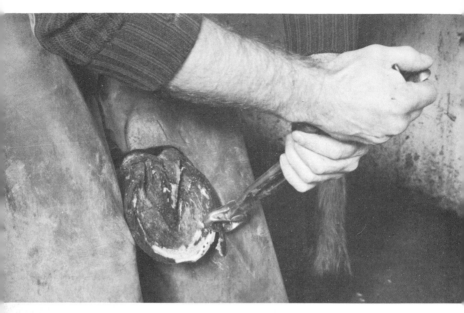

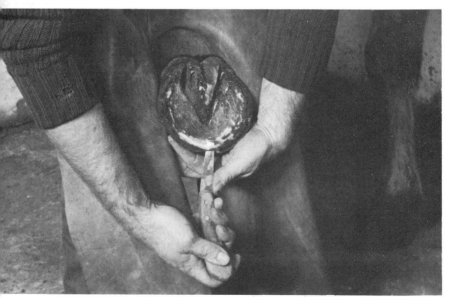

Figs. 23 and 24 Left: *To assess how much of the wall needs to be removed, the horn is cut away so as to reveal the white line,* above. *It is then trimmed with the drawing knife,* below.

Fig. 25 Below: *Using the rasp the farrier obtains a smooth and level bearing surface.*

needs to be removed to trim the foot to the sole surface, a thin strip of horn is cut from the inside of the wall to reveal the white line. The bearing surface of the foot should then be rasped smooth and level, having regard for the maintenance or correction of the foot-pastern axis.

If the *toe is too long*, the FPA will be broken back at the coronet to put greater strain on the flexor tendons. It is

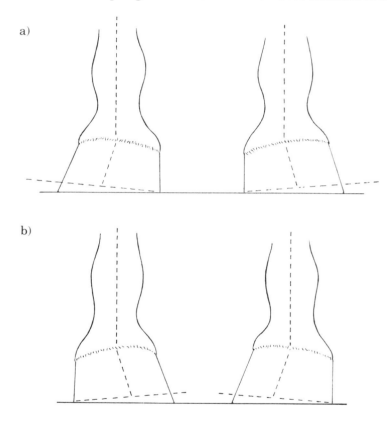

Fig. 26 *Feet which are a) broken inwards, or b) broken outwards have to be corrected before the fitting of the shoe. In the first instance there is excessive growth on the outside of the hoof, in the second there is too much growth on the inside.*

corrected by careful shortening of the toe. Should the *heels be too high*, the FPA is broken forward at the coronet, causing extra weight to be put on the toe and reducing pressure on the frog. A correction is made by lowering the heels.

When the *heels are too low*, extra weight is put on the back of the foot and the tendons are subjected to strain. To restore the axis it is necessary to lower the quarters and toe.

Should there be more than normal growth on one side of the foot, or if one side is lower in comparison with the other, the wall has to be lowered on the appropriate side.

Failure to dress, or to prepare, the foot accurately alters the position of the latter in relation to the joints of the lower limb, producing unequal stresses and interfering with the normal action.

FAULTS IN PREPARATION

☐ Over-lowering the wall. The fault, though rare, is usually associated with flat-footed horses.

☐ Uneven bearing surface – one side lower than the other.

☐ Dumping the toe, a serious fault caused by rasping the toe rather than shortening the foot by rasping the ground surface. Dumping reduces the bearing surface and, by removing the hard, outer horn, exposes the softer layers beneath which then become brittle. (Dumping is occasionally permissible to a limited extent with flat feet, in order to get the nails high enough up the wall to be secure.)

☐ Paring the frog and sole. Removal of the frog destroys the natural function so that it becomes shrivelled. Cutting away the sole reduces its strength and makes it susceptible to bruising.

☐ Opening the heels – i.e. cutting away the bars to make the foot look wider. This causes the wall to turn inwards, reduces the ability to absorb concussion and leads to contraction.

FITTING THE SHOE

Once the surface and outline of the shoe correspond with those of the foot, the shoe can be nailed on. The first nail to

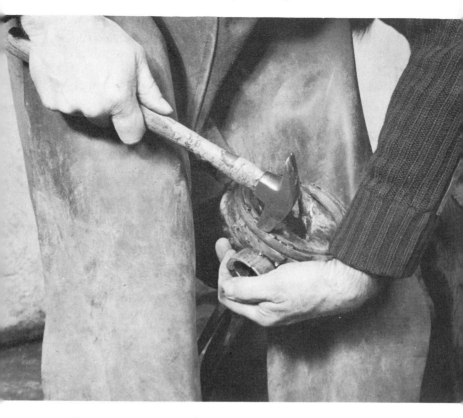

Fig. 27 *Clenches are made by holding the pincers against the nail stubs and then driving the nail heads home.*

be driven in is usually at the toe, but it may just as frequently be the inside heel nail. Each nail is angled to come through the wall about one third of the way up, and the protruding point is twisted off. The remainder of the shank forms the clench.

Clenches are made by pushing the jaws of the pincers upwards against the stubs and driving the heads home with the hammer. The nails thus secure the shoe to the foot, and the stubs, when turned over, become clenches.

The clenches should be rasped to an even length, beginning from the inside of the foot. A small groove can be cut beneath them with the rasp edge, the pincers are then held under the heads and the clenches bedded into the groove with the hammer before being smoothed off.

MISDIRECTED NAILS

The most common accidents are *pricks* caused by misdirected nails penetrating or 'binding' upon the sensitive

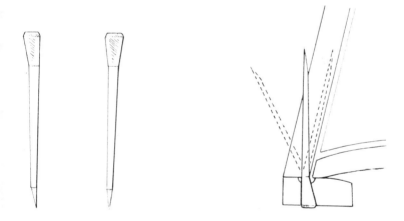

Fig. 28   *The standard horseshoe nail has a countersunk head and two faces, the outer face being straight. The nail is always driven with the outer face to the outside.*

foot, which result in temporary lameness. The farrier must inform the horse's owner. If treated with an antiseptic a 'prick' will usually not give further trouble.

A *nail bind* is when the nail is driven too close to the sensitive structure. It causes pressure, pain and lameness, although the effects of these may be delayed. The offending nail should be withdrawn and the horse rested for two or three days.

THE FINISHED FOOT

The following points should be observed:

☐ Front and hind feet must be exact pairs (in size, shape and foot-pastern axis).

☐ No dumping.

☐ No rasping other than below the clenches.

☐ Clenches in line: approximately one third of the way up the wall and parallel with the coronary band rather than the ground, even and flat.

☐ Clips must be flat, low and broad. Toe clip must be central.

☐ Shoe must fit the outline of the foot.

☐ Heels of shoes must be of correct length. Where the heels of the front shoes are too long they can be trodden on by the hind foot and the shoe pulled off. Long heels will also cause capped elbows: the heel of the shoe rubbing the point of the elbow when the horse lies down.

If the heels are too short, some of the bearing surface is lost and as the foot grows they put pressure on the seat of corn.

Front shoes should be fitted so as to extend very slightly beyond the horn and should then be bevelled in line with the angle of the heels. For horses in fast work, the heels should terminate just short of the end of the horn and should then be bevelled off obliquely.

When the foot is lifted:

☐ Nails must be driven home, flush with the shoe.

☐ Frog or sole must not be pared.

☐ Heels must not be opened.

☐ On forefeet toe clip must be in line with point of frog.

☐ No gap between foot and shoe which would indicate unevenness of one or other surface.

☐ No interference with the frog.

The horse should always be trotted out so that any signs of lameness or unlevel action can be detected.

5

Corrective and Surgical Shoeing

Corrective shoeing is necessary for dealing with injuries sustained through the ill effects of shoes, for defective feet, and for imperfect action. Specific diseases of the foot may be alleviated by surgical shoeing carried out according to the recommendations of the veterinary surgeon.

CORRECTIVE SHOEING
The more common problems requiring this remedy are injury, defective feet, imperfect action.

Injury
CAPPED ELBOW. This is a soft swelling on the point of the elbow, caused by the shoe being brought into contact with the elbow when the horse is lying down. It is aggravated by uneven floors and insufficient bedding, which can cause the elbow to be struck as the horse is getting up.

The foot should be shod with a short, narrow inner heel, rasped off and rounded in a spoon shape. The fitting of a *sausage boot* round the pastern will also provide a satisfactory solution.

Defective Feet
FLAT FLEET are often large, with an excessive slope to the wall and low heels. The sole is flat rather than concave. A *seated-out* shoe is used to ease pressure on the sole (see Chapter 3).
TWISTED FEET are either a congenital defect or are caused by faulty shoeing. The latter can be put right, but in the

case of malformations it is only possible to prevent them from becoming worse. Usually the bearing surface of the foot is unlevel, with more growth on the straighter inner wall. It can be corrected by lowering the wall (which will take time) until a level surface is obtained. The shoe should be fitted to conform with the *normal* outline not to that of the twisted foot.

UPRIGHT FEET (also known as 'boxy' or 'mule' feet.) The wall is straight, the heels are high, and the frog is small and shrivelled. The remedy is to dress the foot so as to maintain a proper foot-pastern axis. Special shoes are not required.

LOW HEELS occur when the wall curves inwards under the sole. The condition is made worse by pressure from the shoe. The curved-in portion of the heel has to be cut down until the foot carries weight evenly.

Correction may be attempted with a *bar shoe*. This is a shoe joined by a bar at the heels which causes pressure to be transferred to the frog. It must be used carefully, as the pressure is abnormal and should be sustained for only short periods.

CONTRACTED FEET. Characteristically the contracted foot is small, very narrow at the heels, and has an atrophied frog. It may be caused by disease, injury leading to disablement or disuse, or possibly by bad dressing of the foot.

The horse can be worked in *tips*, covering only the fore-part of the foot, so that the weight is taken on the rear. Alternatively the farrier may consider grooving the foot to obtain expansion.

If the cause is an incurable condition nothing can be done.

Imperfect Action

BRUSHING. This is the term applied when the inside of one leg is struck with the opposite foot. It occurs generally in the area of the fetlock.

A *feather-edge* shoe often provides a solution. The inside

branch is narrowed and made higher than the outer one in an effort to throw the foot outward from the usual line of flight.

SPEEDY-CUTTING. This is an injury to the foreleg in the area of the knee, caused by a blow from the inner toe or edge of the opposite shoe while the horse is travelling at speed. Imbalance is a contributing factor, and injuries often occur when the horse leads with the wrong leg or is changing the leading leg.

The usual remedy is a shoe with the inner branch, from toe to quarter, well narrowed and fitted well under the foot.

OVER-REACHING. An over-reach is an injury to the foreleg between knee and heel caused by a blow from the toe of the hind foot. It occurs when galloping, jumping, or crossing deep ground.

An injury above the fetlock is a 'high over-reach'; one below, commonly on the bulbs of the heels, is a 'low over-reach.' Horses with long legs and short bodies are most prone to over-reaching. It is also aggravated when the horse is tired and/or unfit.

To encourage the forefeet to move out of the way, or to break-over, more quickly, the feet are kept short, the toe of the shoe is rolled and the heels are raised. To delay the break-over in the hind feet, the heels of the shoe are left a little long and are graduated so as to be thinner than the toe. The shoe is set well back and well rounded off.

FORGING or CLACKING. This describes the striking of the front shoe with the toe of the hind foot. Apart from the irritation of the continual noise, there is a danger of the front shoe being pulled off, causing the horse to stumble or fall.

A *dub-toed* hind shoe – i.e. the toe squared, well rounded off, and set well back – will often eliminate the fault.

STUMBLING. A horse stumbles by catching a front toe or by failing to clear the ground sufficiently. Tiredness, over-long feet, or stiffness in the joints are all reasons for stumbling.

Horses are more likely to stumble when newly shod and before the shoe has become worn in.

A *rolled toe* shoe will usually give satisfactory results, but the degree to which the shoe is 'set up' will depend on how the horse stumbles (which can be discovered by examining the used shoe) and the reasons for his doing so.

DRAGGING TOE. A horse may drag a hind toe because of lameness or stiffness in the quarters or hock joint, or because he is unfit.

A rolled toe shoe is not in itself a cure, but the shoe will wear longer.

SURGICAL SHOEING

CORNS. A corn is a bruise between the wall and the bars of the foot – the 'seat of corn' – and is caused by pressure from shoes which have been left on too long or which are too short in the heel. It occurs in the forefeet.

Corns are recognised by red discoloration of the horn. They can be *dry*, *moist*, or *suppurating* when infected.

In the majority of cases it will be sufficient to pare down the discoloured portion of the sole, rest the horse for a few days, and then refit an ordinary shoe, taking great care to ensure a correct fitting on the wall and bar areas. In more severe cases, when infection is present, veterinary assistance will be required to cut away the affected part of the sole. Poulticing may be necessary, and any subsequent cavity will need to be packed with tow and Stockholm tar to prevent further infection.

LAMINITIS is a painful inflammation of the sensitive laminae in the toe areas. It generally occurs in the forefeet, but the hind feet can also be affected. The most common cause is a diet too rich for the individual metabolism, combined with overweight and a lack of exercise. Ponies on summer grass are particularly susceptible. Changes occur in the shape of the foot and are due largely to the rotation of the third phalanx and the dropping of the sole.

Special shoes will help to relieve pain. Those commonly recommended are a *seated-out* shoe, for mild attacks of the disease, or a *rocker-bar* shoe.

NAVICULAR. This is a general term referring to inflammation of the navicular bursae and/or erosion of the navicular bone. Lameness is at first intermittent but becomes chronic. The horse points his toe forward, raising his heel to alleviate the pain.

Modern veterinary drugs and remedial shoeing may keep the horse sound for a considerable period of time.

A *wide web* shoe, fitted long and wide to support the rear of the foot, or an *egg bar* shoe, flat and extending beyond the bulbs of the heel, will be helpful and will do something to restore a proper foot-pastern axis.

SANDCRACK. A *true* sandcrack is a split in the wall starting at the coronary band and extending downwards. Classification is according to position and the degree to which the crack has travelled down the wall. Cracks are described as *toe* or *quarter sandcracks* and as being either *complete* or *incomplete*. If the sensitive foot is involved the horse will be seriously lame.

Cases frequently occur in dry, hot weather when the horn is brittle or if the periople has been destroyed by rasping. The sandcrack appears suddenly, usually when galloping on hard surfaces.

Treatment consists of clipping or nailing the crack together, burning a groove across it, or removing a V-shape piece to take pressure off the base of the wall around the crack. An ordinary shoe with clips drawn on either side of the crack will help to prevent it opening.

A *false sandcrack* is a split in the bottom of the wall travelling upwards. It occurs when horn is dry and brittle or when feet are otherwise neglected. Usually, false cracks can be cut out when the feet are trimmed, or a groove can be burned to prevent the crack developing upwards.

SEEDY TOE. This is the result of a separation of the sensitive and insensitive laminae at the toe. A cavity is formed which becomes filled with crumbling horn.

The degenerate horn has to be cleared and the cavity packed with Stockholm tar and tow or cotton wool. A plain shoe with a wide web at the toe is used to protect the bearing surface and to retain the dressing.

SIDEBONE. This is a disease caused by the ossification of the lateral cartilages. It is hereditary, but concussion is accepted as a contributory factor.

The new shoe will be made in exactly the same shape as the worn one, and will be gradually thinner on the affected side, with the width of the web increasing to support the outline of the bulging coronet.

Horses with bi-lateral sidebone wear the toe hard, so a rolled toe shoe will be needed, with graduated, raised heels.

SPAVIN. This is of two types: *bog* spavin and *bone* spavin. Both affect the hock joint.

Bog spavin is a soft swelling high on the inside of the joint and can usually be dispersed with rest.

Bone spavin is an arthritic condition of the hock joint which causes pain, swelling and heat. The flexion of the joint is reduced, and there is a characteristic dragging of the toe.

A thick, rolled toe shoe is used. It has raised heels to ease the joint and to facilitate its action. Long, sloping heels, allowing the horse to slide the foot, help to reduce jarring.

CURB. This is a sprain of the plantar ligament resulting in a swelling under the point of the hock joint. Shoeing with a rolled toe and raised heel as for spavin will help to reduce strain in the ligament.

TENDON STRAIN occurs generally in the superficial and deep tendons of the legs following severe stress.

Lameness and pain are relieved by raising the heels of the shoes to reduce the tension on the tendons or, in severe cases, by employing a *Patten* shoe.

PADS-CUSHIONS-WEDGES

Pads and cushions are sometimes used to protect the sole and/or to reduce concussion.

PADS may be made of leather, rubber or plastic. They are about ³⁄₁₆ inch (4 mm) thick, cover the whole foot, and are kept in place by the shoe.

They may be used for flat or bruised soles, puncture wounds, or *pedalostitis* (inflammation on the pedal bone edge). The foot should be packed with tow and Stockholm tar before the pads are fitted. Continual use of pads is not recommended as they cause the frog to atrophy.

CUSHIONS are rubber or plastic pads moulded to the shape of the foot and secured by the shoe. They give protection and absorb concussion, but should not be used continually.

HEEL WEDGES are graduated pads made to fit under the heel of the shoe in order to raise it by about ¼ inch or 6 mm. There is a danger of disturbing a correct foot-pastern axis but they can help to achieve a better angle when the conformation of hoof or pastern is poor.

Care of the Feet

STABLED HORSES

Care of the feet in the stabled horse involves:

● The maintenance of *stable hygiene* at all times. The stable and bed must be kept scrupulously clean.

● *The cleanliness of the feet.* Feet should be picked out twice daily, morning and evening, and also when the horse returns from work. Picking out involves the *thorough* cleaning of the foot. In particular the space between shoe and sole and the clefts of the frog should be kept free of dirt and grit.

● The maintenance of *moisture content.* With horses stabled for long periods the foot is unable to make good the loss of moisture caused by evaporation. The foot therefore becomes dry, brittle and prone to cracking.

Moisture can be replaced by daily washing. Hard bristle brushes should *not* be used as they can remove the essential periople.

Hoof oil or *ointment* helps to retain moisture and should therefore be applied *after* exercise or turning out: if it is used before, the waterproof coating formed on the hoof prevents moisture being absorbed. The principles relative to hoof dressings and their effect upon the moisture content, which apply to both stabled horses and those at grass are as follows:

☐ *Under normal conditions* continuous application of impervious dressings to the hoof prevents evaporation which causes the horn to become soft.

☐ *In wet conditions* the opposite occurs. The dressing counters any excessive absorption of moisture and thus prevents the horn from being softened.

☐ *In dry conditions*, dressings will prevent loss of the moisture content and if brittle feet are soaked in water and then dressed with oil or ointment, the application will help to retain it.

• *Regular removal of shoes*, the shoes being replaced when necessary. Shoes should be removed every 4 to 5 weeks to remove growth and to re-establish the foot-pastern axis.

THRUSH. This can occur in both the stabled horse and in one kept at grass. It indicates a failure in management, and arises when conditions under foot are wet and dirty and when regular inspection of the feet is neglected.

Thrush is a disease of the frog caused by the breakdown of the horn and characterised by a foul-smelling discharge. In advanced cases it is necessary to cut out the infected part and to pack the cavity with Stockholm tar.

HORSES AT GRASS

The practice of removing shoes from horses turned out during the summer (or at any time) is beneficial, as it enables the hooves to grow without interference from nails.

Daily examination of the feet is still essential, and they should be dressed professionally, and as frequently as those of the shod horse so as to preserve the foot-pastern axis and to control normal growth.

TIPS, or HALF-SHOES, are sometimes fitted to horses before they are turned out. They prevent the toes from being worn and allow the rear part of the frog to bear the weight normally. However, constant supervision is required, as tips easily become loose.

Youngstock

It is essential to pay particular attention to the feet of

youngstock which in their formative stage can easily develop defects.

Common occurrences, easily checked if dealt with in the early stages, are for *toes to turn in or out*. When toes are turned in, the overgrowth occurs on the inside wall. This has to be rasped level if the action is to be corrected. The opposite happens with a foot is turned out and it is then the outside wall which must be levelled.

Where the wall in front becomes straightened and the heels raised – a common enough defect in young horses – it is possible for the flexor tendon to become contracted unless remedial measures are promptly taken. The treatment involves no more than taking down the heels to restore the balance of the foot.

7

Preparing for the Farrier

The following simple guidelines should help to save you, and your farrier, time and trouble.

☐ Make arrangements for the farrier's visit in advance so that he can plan his itineraries.

☐ Warn him if anything unusual has occurred since his last visit.

☐ Make sure that your horse will stand still whilst being shod. An unruly horse, as well as being dangerous, wastes time and makes it difficult for the farrier to do a good job. *The responsibility for training the horse rests with the owner not the farrier.*

☐ Have the horse clean and ready for the farrier when he arrives.

☐ Be able to measure the size of shoe required.

☐ Provide a suitable safe area free from obstructions, and preferably under cover.

☐ If the horse is to be shod 'hot', make sure that all combustible materials are removed from the area.

☐ Be at hand to hold the horse's head.

If the horse is to be shod at the farrier's forge, arrive there in good time, with a rug to put over the horse if necessary. Aim to arrive with the horse calm, dry and clean. He will not stand quietly if you have hurried him.

8

Control and Qualifications

The Farriers Registration Acts of 1975 and 1977 make it unlawful in Britain for anyone to shoe a horse unless he/she is listed in the Register of Farriers. It is unlawful for any person not in the Register to describe him/herself as a farrier or shoeing smith. The object of the Act is to prevent unskilled persons from shoeing horses and to avoid animals being subjected either to cruelty or suffering caused by inexpert attention.

☐ Before employing a farrier, horse-owners should ensure that he is properly registered.

☐ The Worshipful Company of Farriers has special responsibilities to promote education and training in farriery, and ensures the maintenance of standards through its role as the examining body.

☐ A system of apprentice training, evolved with the collaboration of a number of interested bodies, exists in Britain. The farriery apprenticeship, involving a probationary period with an approved training farrier, is of four years duration and apprentices are not allowed to shoe horses except under the supervision of the training farrier.

☐ The Register consists of four parts – entry to any one being according to qualification and experience.

PART 1. Farriers who have completed a four-year apprenticeship and have passed the RSS or Dip. WCF examinations or the Army Trade Test. Such farriers may also hold higher qualifications.

PART 2. Farriers with a minimum of two years in business as a farrier.

PART 3. Horse-owners who have regularly and competently shod their own horses or horses belonging to other persons without reward. It is unlawful for persons registered in this grade to shoe for gain or reward.

PART 4. Farriers who have had two years regular and gainful engagement in shoeing horses whilst being otherwise employed and shoeing as a part-time occupation.

The closing date for applications to be included in these parts of the register closed in 1980.

The examinations in farriery held by the Worshipful Company of Farriers are as follows:

DIPLOMA WCF. 1st grade attempted after 3½ years apprenticeship.

AWCF (ASSOCIATE). 2nd Grade attempted after a *minimum* of two years further experience.

FWCF (FELLOW). Attempted only by Associates of twelve months standing and at least five years after gaining Dip. WCF.

Only holders of the FWCF may be appointed as examiners in farriery.

Index

Figures in *italics* refer to illustrations